BRAHMA SUTRA BHĀṢYA - SHANKARACHARYA'S DEFINING WORK

Brahma Sutra Bhāṣya - Shankaracharya's Defining Work

DR SURABHI SOLANKI

First Printing, 2025

Contents

Preface

"Brahman is real; the world is an appearance; the Self is not different from Brahman." — Ādi Shankaracharya

Across centuries, humanity has sought the same truth through different mirrors — science, art, philosophy, and faith. The question behind every pursuit has remained unchanged: *Who am I, and what is this vast reality I inhabit?* The **Brahma Sutras** — concise aphorisms composed by Sage Bādarāyaṇa — are among the most profound attempts to systematize that inquiry.

But the Sutras themselves are enigmatic: cryptic, dense, and open to interpretation. It was **Ādi Shankaracharya**, in the 8th century CE, who breathed life into their silence. His *Bhāṣya* (commentary) became not merely an explanation but a **philosophical revolution** — one that unified the diverse streams of Indian thought under the vision of **Advaita (non-duality)**.

Today, as we navigate a hyperconnected yet fragmented world — where identities multiply and meaning scatters — Shankara's message regains its urgency. *Advaita* is not escapism; it is radical clarity. It teaches that consciousness alone is real and that everything else — all differences, desires, and fears — arise and dissolve within it, like waves upon the ocean.

This book seeks to **re-present Shankara's Brahma Sutra Bhāṣya for the modern seeker** — not by simplifying it, but by contextualizing it. We will explore its philosophical depth alongside its relevance to science, psychology, and spiritual practice.

You will not merely read Shankara here; you will walk with him — through his logic, compassion, and fierce devotion to truth.

Love and reverence,
Surabhi Solanki
Uttarakhand
India

Why the Brahma Sutras Matter Today

The Eternal Quest

Every civilization reaches a point where outer progress demands an inner response. The Brahma Sutras begin exactly there — with the phrase:

"Athāto Brahma Jijñāsā" — *"Now, therefore, the inquiry into Brahman."*

This "Now" is not chronological; it is existential. It arises when the soul, tired of transient pleasures, turns inward. When Shankara comments on this line, he invites us into a spiritual maturity — a readiness to question the very ground of our being.

In our age of digital noise and constant distraction, the **call of Jijñāsā — the longing to know** — is revolutionary. It reminds us that wisdom is not in acquiring data, but in dissolving doubt.

Shankara's Radical Vision

Shankara's commentary is not just metaphysical poetry; it's **methodical dismantling** of illusion. He analyzes rival schools — from Buddhism to Nyāya — with precision and respect, showing that the diversity of doctrines points toward a single underlying truth.

For him, *Advaita* is not a belief but an insight: **that the knower, the known, and the act of knowing are one.**

This recognition does not negate the world but redefines it — as a shimmering appearance of the infinite consciousness we call Brahman.

Why the Sutras Still Speak

In a postmodern, pluralistic world, many feel unanchored. The Brahma Sutras remind us that truth is not relative; **it is relational** — not found "out there" but realized "in here."

The age of artificial intelligence, neuroscience, and quantum physics has made Shankara's message newly resonant. When physicists say that matter and energy are inseparable, and mystics say that self and world are one — they echo the same insight from different doorways.

The Need for a New Commentary

To modern readers, the Brahma Sutra Bhāṣya can appear forbiddingly abstract. Yet, beneath its dialectic, it carries immense compassion — for the human struggle to know, to belong, to be free.

This retelling aims to be **a bridge between tradition and transformation**:

- Preserving Shankara's logic and linguistic precision.
- Translating metaphysical insights into psychological clarity.
- Showing how the non-dual perspective can heal our fractured sense of self and society.

A Living Inquiry

The Sutras end where they begin — in the mystery of awareness itself. The journey from ignorance (*Avidyā*) to liberation (*Moksha*) is not an escape from the world but an awakening within it.

In reading the Brahma Sutra Bhāṣya today, we are not studying ancient scripture — we are **studying ourselves.**
And if Shankara's words still breathe, it is because they were never about him; they were about the truth that lives through all of us.

The Spiritual Landscape Before Shankara

The Age of Inquiry

Long before Shankara walked the lands of Bhārata, the Indian subcontinent was already a **university of ideas**. Philosophers debated under banyan trees, kings sponsored schools of thought, and monks traversed from Kashmir to Kanyakumari seeking realization.

It was an era not of dogma, but of **dialogue**. Every thinker asked: *What is real? What is the self? What is liberation?*

From this questioning arose six great systems — the *Ṣaḍ-darśanas* — each gazing upon truth from a distinct lens:

1. **Nyāya** – Logic and epistemology.
2. **Vaiśeṣika** – Atomism and realism.
3. **Sāṃkhya** – Dualism between consciousness and matter.
4. **Yoga** – Discipline and union through practice.
5. **Pūrva Mīmāṃsā** – Ritual precision and moral order.
6. **Vedānta** – The culmination: reflection upon the Upanishads.

Shankara's *Bhāṣya* belongs to the last of these — but it integrates the clarity of all.

The Shadow of Duality

The centuries before Shankara were marked by a **spiritual fragmentation**. Buddhism and Jainism had offered rational alternatives to ritual orthodoxy, questioning the authority of the Vedas. The Buddha's compassion and clarity had spread across Asia, while Hindu thinkers struggled to reconcile devotion, reason, and revelation.

Out of this tension emerged a deeper question:
If all phenomena are impermanent and devoid of self, as the Buddha said — then **who** seeks liberation?
And if the Vedas proclaim "Tat Tvam Asi" — *Thou art That* — what is this *Thou* that equals the infinite?

The air was charged with intellectual energy — and existential unease. The human longing for permanence met the philosopher's demand for proof.

The Seeds of Vedānta

The **Upanishads** — ancient dialogues between seers and seekers — had already hinted at the truth Shankara would later crystallize. They spoke of:

- **Brahman**: the unchanging reality underlying all things.
- **Ātman**: the inner self, pure consciousness.
- **Moksha**: liberation through the realization of their unity.

Yet their language was poetic, intuitive, and open-ended. Over centuries, interpretations multiplied.

Sage **Bādarāyaṇa**, author of the *Brahma Sutras*, sought to bring order — codifying the scattered insights of the Upanishads into 555 concise aphorisms.

But even the Sutras themselves became battlefields of meaning.

The Many Schools of the One Truth

By Shankara's time, **multiple interpretations** of the Brahma Sutras had emerged:

- **Bhāskara's** *Bhedābheda* (difference and non-difference).
- **Rāmānuja's** later *Vishishtādvaita* (qualified non-dualism).
- **Madhva's** eventual *Dvaita* (dualism).

Each claimed fidelity to the Vedas — yet diverged radically in metaphysics. Was Brahman personal or impersonal? Was the world real or illusionary? Was the soul identical with or subordinate to God?

India was not at war, but it was **arguing about reality** — and these debates shaped theology, art, and ethics alike.

The Birth of a Synthesizer

Into this chorus of voices stepped **Ādi Shankaracharya**, a youth from Kalady, Kerala — serene, brilliant, and destined to redefine the conversation.

He saw that truth was being fragmented by the very intellect that sought it. The path back to unity, he realized, lay not in new doctrines but in **direct realization**.

Where others saw opposites — ritual and renunciation, form and formlessness, faith and reason — Shankara saw continuity. To him, the world was neither to be denied nor adored — it was to be *understood*.

Thus began the composition of his commentaries — on the *Upanishads*, *Bhagavad Gītā*, and the *Brahma Sutras* — together forming the **Prasthāna Traya Bhāṣya**.

But among these, the *Brahma Sutra Bhāṣya* became the foundation — the intellectual and spiritual skeleton of Advaita Vedānta.

The Need for Integration

In retrospect, Shankara's work was not merely scholastic; it was **civilizational repair**.

He reconciled Vedic authority with rational inquiry, yogic experience with metaphysical clarity, and the inward journey with the external order of dharma.

His synthesis ensured that Indian spirituality would not collapse into sectarianism or skepticism. He anchored it in the **timeless self-awareness** that transcends both belief and disbelief.

Through his vision, the chaos of doctrines became the **cosmos of consciousness**.

The Dawn Before the Light

Before Shankara, the philosophical horizon was radiant with scattered stars — luminous but unconnected.

With Shankara, they became a **constellation** — the Advaitic cosmos, where every question finds its center in the self.

The stage was set.

The world awaited a teacher who would silence centuries of confusion with the simple truth:

"Brahman alone is real, the world is appearance, and the Self is not different from Brahman."

The Life and Genius of Ādi Shankaracharya

The Child of the River

In a quiet village called **Kalady**, nestled on the banks of the river *Poorna* in Kerala, a miracle was born in the 8th century CE. The child, **Shankara**, came to the devout couple Shivaguru and Aryamba after years of prayer to Lord Shiva. His birth was seen as the grace of the Divine — not for their family alone, but for the world.

From an early age, Shankara displayed an uncanny intellect. The boy who could chant the *Vedas* by heart soon began asking questions that silenced elders. At eight, he grasped the subtleties of Sanskrit grammar and philosophy that others studied for decades. But more than brilliance, he radiated **detachment** — a rare stillness that no toy or comfort could disturb.

The Call of Renunciation

Legend tells that one day, while bathing in the river, Shankara was seized by a crocodile. In that mortal moment, he asked his mother for permission to renounce worldly life. Aryamba, moved by both terror and love, granted his wish.

Miraculously, the crocodile released him — as if nature itself had waited for that vow.

Thus began his journey as a **sannyāsin** — a monk at the tender age of eight. He left home, not out of rebellion, but realization. His renunciation was not escape; it was **alignment** — a surrender to the higher order of truth.

In his *Bhāṣya*, he would later write,

"Renunciation is not abandonment of action, but of attachment."

And his life became the living commentary of those words.

Meeting the Guru

Shankara's search for a teacher led him to the sage **Govindapāda**, who dwelt in meditation on the banks of the Narmada. The story of their meeting is luminous: the boy approached the cave, bowed, and chanted a spontaneous hymn — declaring that though waves may rise and fall, the ocean remains unchanged.

Hearing this, Govindapāda recognized the young seeker as the one foretold — a soul destined to revive the essence of Vedānta. Under his guidance, Shankara immersed himself in deep study of the *Upanishads*, *Yoga*, and *Samkhya* — mastering not only the texts, but the **spirit of inquiry** behind them.

When the time came, Govindapāda gave him the mission that would define his life:

"Go forth, and re-establish the wisdom of the Upanishads — that the Self alone is Brahman."

The Teacher Who Walked the Land

What followed was a journey unlike any in history.

Shankara, barely in his teens, began walking across India — barefoot, carrying only his staff and manuscripts. He debated philosophers, monks, and scholars in temples and courts, not to win, but to **illuminate**.

He traversed from **Kedarnath to Kanchipuram, Dwarka to Puri**, uniting the land not by conquest, but by **conversation**. Everywhere he went, he left behind clarity — a reordering of chaos into coherence.

To institutionalize his vision, he founded the **four monastic centers (Mathas)**:

- **Sringeri** in the South — preserving knowledge.
- **Dwaraka** in the West — representing strength.
- **Puri** in the East — upholding devotion.
- **Badrinath** in the North — symbolizing renunciation.

These became the four **pillars of Advaita**, ensuring that India's spiritual compass would forever point toward unity.

Dialogues that Shaped Destiny

Shankara's journey was not without confrontation. He met thinkers from every school — from ritualists to Buddhists — engaging in debates that were both sharp and compassionate.

His legendary dialogue with **Mandana Mishra**, a scholar devoted to ritual philosophy, is particularly symbolic. Their debate lasted days, moderated by Mandana's wife, Ubhaya Bharati — herself a scholar and embodiment of Saraswati.

When Mandana finally accepted defeat, he became Shankara's disciple, taking the name **Sureshvara**. The encounter wasn't about victory; it was **integration** — reason bowing to realization.

Shankara showed that Advaita did not reject diversity; it **transcended it**. Every path — devotion, knowledge, or action — could lead to the same summit if stripped of ego.

The Bhāṣyas and Beyond

In a life that spanned barely **three decades**, Shankara wrote commentaries on the *Upanishads*, the *Bhagavad Gītā*, and the *Brahma Sutras*.

Among these, the *Brahma Sutra Bhāṣya* stood supreme — a masterpiece of reasoning that transformed Vedānta into a precise philosophy.

Each line reveals a synthesis of **logic and illumination**. Shankara doesn't merely explain the Sutras — he uses them as mirrors to reflect the unity of existence.

He also composed hymns — *Bhaja Govindam*, *Nirvāṇa Ṣaṭkam*, *Saundarya Lahari* — showing that **pure reason and pure devotion** spring from the same source.

To him, the intellect was a bridge to transcendence, not its obstacle.

The Final Silence

Tradition holds that Shankara left his mortal body at **Kedarnath** at the age of 32, disappearing into the Himalayas like a wave returning to the sea.

No one saw death; they saw **dissolution into the Absolute**.

He came, not to start a religion, but to remind us that there was never more than one reality — and that reality is consciousness itself.

Shankara's genius was not only in his words, but in his silence — the silence of a mind that had realized there was never a separation to begin with.

The Legacy of the Living Flame

More than a thousand years later, Shankara's fire still burns. It burns in the monk's meditation, the scholar's thought, the scientist's curiosity, and the seeker's longing.

He proved that **spirituality and intellect are not rivals but reflections** — each completing the other.

In an age that oscillates between skepticism and blind faith, Shankara stands as the middle path: **the path of inquiry that ends in realization**.

He taught that enlightenment is not a mystical event but the *recognition of what already is.*
In that recognition, the universe itself awakens.

The Philosophical Foundations of Advaita Vedānta

This chapter will distill the essence of Shankara's metaphysical framework — the scaffolding that holds the entire *Bhāṣya* together — and interpret it in light of modern science, psychology, and consciousness studies.

The Search for the Unchanging

Every human being, knowingly or not, seeks permanence. Amid birth and death, love and loss, success and sorrow — something in us whispers: *There must be that which does not change.*

For Shankara, this quest was not sentimental but scientific. He began where all inquiry must begin — with **experience**. If everything we perceive changes, there must be an **unchanging knower** who witnesses the change. That witness — unconditioned, self-luminous, and indivisible — is **Ātman**, the true Self.

And that very Self, says the Upanishad, is **Brahman** — the infinite consciousness underlying all existence.

"Ayam ātmā brahma" — "This Self is Brahman." (Mandukya Upanishad 2)

This statement is not metaphysical poetry; it is **an equation of identity**.

Just as modern physics equates matter and energy, Advaita equates consciousness and existence.

Brahman — The Absolute Reality

Shankara describes **Brahman** as *"Satyam, Jñānam, Anantam" — Truth, Consciousness, Infinity.*

These are not attributes of Brahman; they are Brahman.

- **Satyam (Truth)** – The unchanging substratum beneath appearances.
- **Jñānam (Consciousness)** – Not "knowledge of something," but *the light by which everything is known.*
- **Anantam (Infinity)** – Beyond time, space, and causation.

In the *Brahma Sutra Bhāṣya*, Shankara insists that Brahman is **self-revealed** (*svayam-prakāśa*).

It doesn't need proof, because all proofs shine in its light.

Trying to prove Brahman is like trying to illuminate the sun with a candle.

From a modern standpoint, Brahman aligns with the idea of **pure awareness** — the field from which space, time, and mind arise. Contemporary neuroscience explores consciousness as a "hard problem"; Shankara saw it as the **only problem worth solving**.

Ātman — The Inner Witness

The *Ātman* is not the ego (*ahaṅkāra*), not the mind (*manas*), not the intellect (*buddhi*), nor the senses.

It is that which *knows* all these — the silent witness of thoughts, emotions, and perceptions.

When we say "I slept well," who knew the peace of deep sleep when the mind was absent?
That knower, says Shankara, is *Ātman*, the ever-present consciousness that neither sleeps nor wakes.

In psychological terms, Ātman corresponds not to the "self-concept" but to **pure subjectivity** — the unobjectifiable experiencer.
Modern thinkers like Jung, Husserl, and even quantum physicists have touched the edges of this realization — but Shankara stands at its center.

"The Self is self-luminous; it illumines the intellect and all else."
— *Brahma Sutra Bhāṣya*, 1.1.4

Māyā — The Cosmic Illusion

If Brahman alone exists, why do we perceive multiplicity, conflict, and change?
Shankara answers this through **Māyā** — not as "illusion" in the sense of unreality, but as **misperception** born of ignorance.

Māyā is the power that makes the rope appear as a snake in dim light — the **projective tendency of consciousness** that overlays the real with the unreal.
It doesn't create a false world but veils the truth of unity.

"As long as ignorance persists, the universe appears real; when knowledge dawns, it dissolves like mist before the sun."

In modern metaphors, Māyā resembles **the lens of perception** — shaped by cognition, language, and conditioning.
Neuroscience confirms that what we "see" is not the world itself, but a brain-generated model filtered through expectation and survival.
Shankara anticipated this millennia ago: the world we take as absolute is, in fact, **a superimposition (adhyāsa)** upon the pure Self.

Avidyā — The Root of Bondage

At the heart of Māyā lies **Avidyā**, ignorance — not absence of knowledge, but **misidentification**.
We mistake the transient for the eternal, the body for the Self, the thought for the thinker.
Avidyā operates through two veils:

1. **Āvaraṇa Śakti** — the power of concealment (hiding Brahman's reality).
2. **Vikṣepa Śakti** — the power of projection (manifesting multiplicity).

Through these, consciousness seems to become the world — and the world seems to obscure consciousness.
Liberation (*moksha*) is not acquisition of new knowledge but **removal of misperception** — like recognizing the rope after mistaking it for a snake.
In psychological language, Avidyā is the **root distortion of identity** — the ego's assumption that it is separate, vulnerable, and incomplete.
All human suffering, says Shankara, arises from this one misunderstanding.

Jīva, Īśvara, and the Mirror of Reality

Advaita does not deny God; it **redefines** God.
When Brahman is viewed through the veil of Māyā, it appears as **Īśvara** — the cosmic intelligence governing creation.
When the same Brahman is reflected in an individual mind, it appears as **Jīva** — the personal self.
Īśvara and Jīva are like reflections of the same sun in different ponds — their brightness varies with the clarity of the water, but the source is one.
The path of Advaita is to realize that both reflections point back to the same **luminosity** — Brahman.
Thus, devotion (*bhakti*) and knowledge (*jñāna*) are not opposed;

they are complementary movements toward the same realization.

The Unity of Opposites

Shankara's vision dissolves dualities without denying their experiential validity:

- Real and unreal.
- Subject and object.
- Transcendence and immanence.

He shows that these are **relative distinctions** within the play of Māyā.

From the standpoint of **Vyāvahārika Satya** (empirical truth), the world functions with order and meaning.

But from the **Pāramārthika Satya** (absolute truth), there is only Brahman — indivisible, unconditioned awareness.

Just as waves differ in form but are one in essence, every being, thought, and atom is Brahman appearing as diversity.

The Psychology of Liberation

For Shankara, enlightenment (*moksha*) is not a future event — it is **the recognition of what already is**.

When ignorance ends, nothing new is attained; rather, the false is removed.

The *Brahma Sutra Bhāṣya* insists that liberation is *jñāna-prāpta*, not *karma-prāpta* — achieved through knowledge, not action.

Yet, this knowledge is not intellectual; it is **existential seeing** — the flash of awareness that *I am That*.

In modern psychological language, this parallels a **radical deconstruction of identity**, where awareness recognizes itself beyond all content — a pure, unmediated consciousness.

When that dawns, the individual no longer seeks peace; they **are peace itself**.

The Science of Oneness

Modern physics whispers echoes of Advaita.

Quantum theory blurs distinctions between observer and observed; relativity dissolves space-time absolutes; neuroscience questions the very locus of the self.

Where science ends in wonder, Shankara begins:

"That which cannot be known by the mind, but by which the mind knows — know That to be the Self." (*Kena Upanishad*)

Advaita is not in conflict with science — it is **its completion**, offering the inner realization of the unity that physics intuits mathematically.

The Foundation Complete

The edifice of the *Brahma Sutra Bhāṣya* stands upon these foundations:

1. **Brahman** — Absolute Reality.
2. **Ātman** — The Self, identical with Brahman.
3. **Māyā/Avidyā** — The veil of illusion.
4. **Moksha** — Liberation through knowledge.

Everything Shankara writes in his commentary is a **refinement of these four pillars**, explored through logic, scripture, and meditation.

In understanding them, we are no longer studying metaphysics — we are studying the architecture of consciousness itself.

"Athāto Brahma Jijñāsā"

"Now, therefore, the inquiry into Brahman."

The Doorway to Truth

The *Brahma Sutras* begin abruptly — no preamble, no background, no promise of heaven.

Just four words: **"Athāto Brahma Jijñāsā."**

It is an invitation.

A knock at the door of the mind.

A quiet challenge: *Are you ready to know the Real?*

This "Now" (*atha*) does not refer to time. It signals **preparedness** — the culmination of moral, intellectual, and emotional maturity. Shankara says that *only when the longing for truth outweighs all other desires* does one truly begin the inquiry into Brahman.

Thus, this first Sutra is both **a beginning and a threshold** — the point where philosophy transforms into direct pursuit of the Infinite.

The Meaning of the Words

Let us break down the Sutra's four terms, as Shankara himself does:

- **Atha (Now):** The auspicious beginning, implying readiness after prior purification — through ethics, study, and self-control.
- **Ataḥ (Therefore):** Indicates logical succession — *therefore*, because of that readiness, the inquiry should begin.
- **Brahma:** The Infinite, the source of creation, sustenance, and dissolution. Not a deity, but **pure Being-Consciousness-Bliss (Sat-Chit-Ānanda)**.
- **Jijñāsā:** The thirst to know — not belief, but *an existential inquiry into reality itself.*

Together they mean:
"Having attained maturity and clarity through prior discipline, one should now inquire into Brahman — the ultimate reality."

Shankara's Vision of Readiness

Shankara is meticulous about what qualifies a seeker for this inquiry. He lists **fourfold qualifications (Sādhana Chatuṣṭaya):**

1. **Viveka** — Discrimination between the eternal and transient.
2. **Vairāgya** — Dispassion toward the fruits of action.
3. **Ṣaṭ-sampatti** — Six inner virtues: calmness, control, endurance, faith, focus, and concentration.
4. **Mumukṣutva** — The burning desire for liberation.

Without these, he warns, the study of Brahman becomes mere intellectual gymnastics — not transformation.
With them, the mind becomes a **mirror polished for truth**.

From Ritual to Realization

The Sutra marks a philosophical revolution.
Before Shankara, many schools equated spirituality with ritual — sacrifice, offerings, mantras.
Shankara gently yet firmly moves the emphasis from **karma (action)** to **jñāna (knowledge)**.

He argues that action, being finite, cannot yield the infinite.
Rituals may purify the mind, but **knowledge alone liberates**.

"Action may remove impurities, but it cannot reveal the sun; only the clouds must part."

This shift was not anti-religious — it was evolutionary.
He preserved the outer path but pointed toward the inner realization it must serve.

In modern terms:
Spirituality begins when **experience takes precedence over tradition**, and inner transformation outweighs outer conformity.

The Psychology of Inquiry

What is *Jijñāsā*, really?
It is not curiosity, but **existential hunger**.
It arises when the soul recognizes that nothing transient can satisfy it.

Modern psychology might call this the "crisis of meaning."
Advaita calls it **grace** — the moment when the false promises of the world collapse, revealing the need for ultimate truth.

Shankara defines this inquiry as *Brahma Jijñāsā*, not *Brahma Vijnāna* (knowledge) — because it begins as seeking, not knowing.
The search itself is sacred, for it purifies the seeker's perception until the truth shines of its own accord.

The Role of Scripture and Reason

Shankara strikes a delicate balance between **Śruti (revealed knowledge)** and **Yukti (reasoning)**.
The inquiry into Brahman, he says, must rely on both:

- *Scripture* provides the map — the Upanishads reveal what reason alone cannot reach.
- *Reason* ensures clarity — it protects faith from blind acceptance.

In the *Bhāṣya*, Shankara writes:
"Scripture reveals Brahman, but reason confirms that revelation."

This harmony of logic and revelation is what made Advaita both **philosophically rigorous and spiritually profound**.
In today's world, it remains a timeless model for integrating science and spirituality.

The Modern Parallel — The Age of Inquiry Reborn

In our age of information, the new "Now" has arrived again.
We have mastered technology, medicine, and communication — but not **meaning**.
We stand, as humanity did in Shankara's time, at the edge of exhaustion — materially abundant yet inwardly hollow.

The Sutra's call — *"Now, therefore, the inquiry into Brahman"* — is the call of the 21st century.
It asks us to turn the instruments of our intellect inward.
To study not the stars, but the seer.
To explore not the atom, but awareness.

The ancient inquiry has become the modern frontier.

From Knowing to Being

For Shankara, knowledge (*jñāna*) is not conceptual; it is **transformative recognition**.

When we inquire into Brahman sincerely, the seeker, the seeking, and the sought dissolve into a single awareness.

This is not an act of discovery but of remembrance.
The truth was never hidden — only overlooked.
Thus, inquiry becomes **meditation**, and meditation becomes **identity**.

"Knowing Brahman is being Brahman." — *Brahma Sutra Bhāṣya, 1.1.1 Commentary*

The Sutra as a Mandala

Each of the four words of the Sutra can be seen as a mandala, a portal:

Word	Symbolic Meaning	Modern Resonance
Atha	The awakening of readiness	The psychological turning point
Ataḥ	The logical consequence	The shift from belief to experience
Brahma	Infinite Consciousness	The Unified Field of awareness
Jijñāsā	Thirst for realization	Existential longing, self-inquiry

Together they form a circle: readiness leads to inquiry; inquiry dissolves the inquirer; what remains is Brahman.

The Beginning That Never Ends

With this single line, Shankara opens not just a scripture but a revolution of consciousness.
Every sutra that follows is an unfolding of this one.
Every commentary, a reflection of this spark.

When the heart is ready and the mind turns inward, "Now" happens — the eternal present where Brahman reveals itself as the Self.

Thus, the *Brahma Sutra Bhāṣya* does not begin in history; it begins in **awareness**.

And in truth, it never ends.

"The purpose of the scriptures is not to tell you what you do not know,
but to remind you of what you have always been."
— *Ādi Shankaracharya*

“Janmādyasya Yataḥ”

“That (Brahman) from which the origin, sustenance, and dissolution of this universe proceed.”

The Definition of the Absolute

The second sutra answers the seeker’s natural question: *What is Brahman?*

Vyāsa (Bādarāyaṇa), the composer of the *Brahma Sutras*, offers a precise yet profound definition:

“**Janmādyasya yataḥ**” — *That from which the birth, continuation, and dissolution of the universe arise, by which it is sustained, and into which it returns — know that to be Brahman.*

This is the **cosmic equation** of Advaita.
It declares that Brahman is both the **source and the substratum**, the **creator and the container** — not as a separate being, but as the very essence of existence itself.

Shankara’s Commentary — The Ground of All

In his *Bhāṣya*, Shankara explains that the Sutra identifies **Brahman as the material and efficient cause** of the universe — the *Upādāna* (that of which something is made) and the *Nimitta* (that by which something is made).

In all worldly examples, the two are different — the potter is not the clay, the goldsmith is not the gold.
But in Brahman, **the creator and the created are one.**

"From Brahman the universe arises, in Brahman it lives, and into Brahman it dissolves — as waves in the ocean."

This dissolves the illusion of separation between *God*, *world*, and *self*.
The pot, the clay, and the artisan are all expressions of the same consciousness.

The Fourfold Causality

Shankara draws from both logic and scripture to establish Brahman as **the total cause** of the cosmos.
He integrates the four traditional forms of causality:

1. **Material Cause (Upādāna)** – Brahman is the substance of which all things are made.
2. **Efficient Cause (Nimitta)** – Brahman is the intelligence that shapes and directs.
3. **Formal Cause (Sādhāraṇa)** – Brahman is the blueprint of order, rhythm, and law.
4. **Final Cause (Prayojana)** – Brahman is the ultimate purpose toward which all evolves.

Thus, nothing exists *outside* Brahman.
The universe is **not a creation ex nihilo (from nothing)** but a **manifestation from fullness (Pūrṇāt Pūrṇam Udacyate)** — as the *Isha Upanishad* proclaims.

The Analogy of Clay and Pot

To illustrate, Shankara invokes a recurring metaphor:

"As all earthen pots are but modifications of clay,
and clay alone is real,
so all names and forms are modifications of Brahman."

The names (*nāma*) and forms (*rūpa*) differ, but the substance is one.
Destruction of the pot is not the end of clay.
Likewise, creation and dissolution are not real changes in Brahman — only changes in **appearance**.

This leads to one of Shankara's boldest conclusions:

"Change belongs to name and form, not to essence."
This is the heart of **non-dual causality** — reality untouched by its own play.

The Source of Order and Intelligence

The Sutra does not merely assert that Brahman is the *origin* of the universe — it implies that **Brahman is intelligence itself**.

The cosmos is not chaotic; it displays purpose, proportion, and intelligence at every level — from the orbits of galaxies to the geometry of a leaf.
Wherever there is order, there must be consciousness.

Shankara writes:

"The designing intelligence of creation cannot arise from inert matter.
Therefore, Brahman, endowed with consciousness, is the cause."

He was not arguing for a *personal God* who designs, but for **consciousness as the organizing principle** of existence — what we might today call *cosmic intelligence* or *universal mind.*

Science and the Sutra — Consciousness as the Source

Modern cosmology tells us that the universe emerged from a singularity — a state beyond space and time.
Quantum theory reveals that matter is not solid but patterns of energy and probability.
Neuroscience admits that consciousness cannot be reduced to the brain.

In all these findings, Shankara's insight echoes:

The universe is a **manifestation**, not a manufacture.

The cause is not outside creation; it **is creation**.

When we look for the origin of reality, we do not find an event — we find **being itself**.

Brahman is that groundless ground.

The Dance of Manifestation

According to Advaita, creation is not a linear act but a **cyclic appearance** — a play (*līlā*) of consciousness within itself.

Just as the mind projects dreams without losing itself, Brahman projects the universe through *Māyā* — appearing as multiplicity while remaining undivided.

Creation (*sṛṣṭi*), preservation (*sthiti*), and dissolution (*pralaya*) are the rhythmic movements of the same awareness.

Nothing is ever truly born or dies — only forms appear and disappear.

As Shankara says:

"From the standpoint of ultimate truth,

there is neither creation nor dissolution — only Brahman."

The Paradox of Creation Without Change

One of Shankara's most subtle arguments is the **doctrine of Vivarta-vāda** — apparent transformation.

When Brahman manifests as the universe, it does not undergo actual modification (*pariṇāma*).

It's like sunlight reflecting through colored glass — the light seems red or blue, but remains white.

Likewise, consciousness seems diverse through the prism of Māyā, yet remains one and unchanged.

This idea anticipates later scientific insights — that **perception is projection**, and reality, in essence, remains untouched by its appearances.

The Inner Universe

The Sutra does not only describe the cosmic order but the **psychological cosmos** within each being.
Just as Brahman projects the universe, the mind projects its personal world of perceptions and memories.

The *macrocosm* (Brahmāṇḍa) and the *microcosm* (Piṇḍāṇḍa) are mirrors of each other.
Understanding the process of creation outwardly helps us decode our creation inwardly — how thoughts arise, persist, and dissolve in the field of awareness.

Thus, the inquiry into the origin of the universe becomes the inquiry into the **origin of the "I."**

The Sutra as Revelation

"Janmādyasya Yataḥ" is not just a statement — it is a **revelation**.
It says:

There is nothing that is not Brahman.
There is no place where consciousness is absent.
There is no moment outside eternity.

Shankara transforms this Sutra into an experiential map:

1. The universe arises — as thought.
2. The universe sustains — through perception.
3. The universe dissolves — into awareness.

When seen rightly, *creation* is not a story of beginnings, but an **unfolding of consciousness knowing itself**.

The Whisper of Modern Insight

Modern thinkers — from Einstein to Schrödinger, from Jung to Bohm — have sensed this truth:
that the observer and the observed, the subject and object, are entangled expressions of one field.

Advaita names that field **Brahman**.
It is not personal, yet intimate; not abstract, yet immediate.

It is the awareness reading these words, the silence between them, and the intelligence that understands them.

The Eternal Return

To realize Brahman is to awaken from the dream of duality. The Sutra tells us that everything returns to its source — not as annihilation, but as **recognition**.

Like a river merging into the ocean, individuality finds its fulfillment in the infinite.
Nothing is lost; only limitation dissolves.

And in that dissolution, the seeker discovers the ultimate paradox:

What we sought was never elsewhere.
What we sought was what we already are.

The Nature of Brahman — Nirguṇa and Saguṇa

The Two Faces of the Infinite

In the previous chapter, we explored *Brahman* as the **source, sustenance, and dissolution** of all creation. But if Brahman is unchanging, how can it appear to create, preserve, and dissolve?

Here, Shankara introduces a vital distinction:
Brahman is **one**, yet appears in **two modes** of perception:

1. **Nirguṇa Brahman** — the formless, attribute-less Absolute.
2. **Saguṇa Brahman** — the same reality reflected through the veil of Māyā, appearing as God, the creator and ruler of the universe.

These are not two Brahmans, but **two ways of knowing** the same truth — as silence and as sound, as ocean and as wave.

Nirguṇa Brahman — The Absolute Beyond All Attributes

Nirguṇa literally means "without qualities."
It does not imply emptiness, but **transcendence** — beyond name, form, time, space, and causation.

In the *Brahma Sutra Bhāṣya*, Shankara writes:

"Brahman is that which is free from all distinctions — of genus, quality, and action."

Nirguṇa Brahman cannot be worshipped, imagined, or described.
It is *pure being* (*Sat*), *pure consciousness* (*Chit*), and *pure bliss* (*Ānanda*).

It is not an object of thought but the **subject of all knowing** — the very awareness in which even the idea of God arises.

Shankara likens it to **the sun**, which shines without effort or intention.
The light does not choose what to illuminate; it simply *is*.

Saguṇa Brahman — The Divine with Attributes

When the same infinite consciousness is viewed through the veil of Māyā, it appears as **Īśvara** — the personal God endowed with attributes: omniscience, omnipotence, and benevolence.

Saguṇa Brahman is Brahman **as experienced by the mind**, clothed in qualities the human heart can relate to — love, wisdom, justice, creation.

Shankara never denies this form.
He honors it as a **pedagogical necessity** — a way for the finite mind to approach the infinite.

"Brahman, reflected in the mirror of Māyā, is Īśvara — the Lord of the universe."

Thus, the God of worship and prayer is not an illusion; it is a **functional truth**, a stepping-stone toward the realization of the ultimate truth.

The Relationship Between the Two

Shankara's insight is profoundly integrative:

- **Nirguṇa Brahman** is the truth as it is.
- **Saguṇa Brahman** is the truth as it appears.

He writes:

"The difference between Nirguṇa and Saguṇa is like that between the ocean at rest and the ocean in waves. The movement does not alter the essence of the water."

When viewed through ignorance (*Avidyā*), Brahman appears as a personal God creating the world.

When viewed through knowledge (*Jñāna*), that same Brahman is seen as **the Self alone**, without second.

Thus, devotion and knowledge are not opposed; they are **successive modes of perception**.

Devotion matures into inquiry, and inquiry culminates in unity.

The Psychology of the Divine

The human mind cannot grasp infinity without form.

That is why Saguṇa Brahman — as *Īśvara*, *Vishnu*, *Shiva*, or *Devi* — becomes an object of **love and surrender**.

Shankara, though a strict non-dualist, composed some of the most beautiful hymns to the divine forms — *Bhaja Govindam*, *Saundarya Lahari*, *Annapūrṇa Stotra* — showing that **intellectual clarity and emotional devotion** can coexist.

He never asks us to abandon worship, but to **understand whom we worship**.

When the heart is purified through devotion, the intellect can awaken to the truth that the deity outside is none other than the Self within.

The Three Levels of Reality

To reconcile these perceptions, Shankara articulates **three orders of reality**:

1. **Pāramārthika Satya** — The Absolute Truth (Nirguṇa Brahman).

2. **Vyāvahārika Satya** — The Empirical Truth (Saguṇa Brahman, world, and individual).
3. **Prātibhāsika Satya** — The Illusory or Dream Reality.

At the highest level, there is only the Absolute — unchanging consciousness.
At the empirical level, the world and God are real **for all practical purposes**.
At the illusory level, individual perceptions distort both.

This hierarchy prevents nihilism. It allows us to live meaningfully in the world while realizing its ultimate unreality.

The Rope and the Snake — Again

To explain the coexistence of Nirguṇa and Saguṇa, Shankara uses his most famous metaphor:

In dim light, a **rope** is mistaken for a **snake**.
The snake (Saguṇa) appears real until the rope (Nirguṇa) is recognized.
Once the truth dawns, the snake is seen as nothing but the rope all along.

Likewise, the personal God and the world are real as long as ignorance persists.
When knowledge dawns, one realizes: **there never was anything but Brahman.**

Science and the Two Perspectives

Modern physics mirrors this duality beautifully:

- At the **macroscopic level**, reality behaves as distinct objects and forces — structured, relational, Saguṇa-like.
- At the **quantum level**, all distinctions blur into a unified field — formless, interpenetrating, Nirguṇa-like.

Just as particles and waves are two aspects of one phenomenon, so are Nirguṇa and Saguṇa two aspects of the same consciousness.

Advaita anticipated this synthesis — not as speculation, but as direct realization.

The Path from Saguṇa to Nirguṇa

Shankara's spiritual psychology outlines a clear evolution:

1. **Karma Yoga** — Purifies the heart through selfless action.
2. **Bhakti Yoga** — Deepens surrender to Saguṇa Brahman.
3. **Jñāna Yoga** — Dissolves duality through inquiry into Nirguṇa Brahman.

Each stage refines the seeker's consciousness.
Devotion transforms emotion into love without demand; knowledge transforms awareness into **identity without division**.

Ultimately, the devotee and the philosopher meet at the same summit — **where the lover disappears into the Beloved.**

The Unity Behind All Forms

To Shankara, all gods, paths, and philosophies are **refractions of the same light**.
He writes:

"As one sun is reflected in many waters,
so one Brahman shines as many deities."

This universality is why Advaita Vedānta could embrace all faiths without fear.
It does not reduce the divine; it **reveals the depth behind its diversity**.

The temple and the telescope, the prayer and the equation — all point to the same mystery: consciousness knowing itself.

The Silence Beyond Worship

At the journey's end, even devotion falls silent.
The worshipper disappears, and what remains is pure awareness.
This is not the negation of God — it is **the fulfillment of God-consciousness**.

In Shankara's words:

"When the mind ceases to distinguish between worshipper and worshipped,
there shines the bliss of Brahman — without second."

That silence is not emptiness. It is the fullness that births all form and all meaning.

The Lesson for the Modern Seeker

Today, the distinction between Nirguṇa and Saguṇa remains profoundly relevant.

- To the scientist: it reveals that matter and consciousness are two sides of one truth.
- To the mystic: it shows that transcendence and immanence are not opposites.
- To the devotee: it reminds that God is not elsewhere, but **within as awareness itself.**

The two are one — **the Absolute dancing as the Relative.**

"Nirguṇam Saguṇam caiva
vyatirekena naiva hi —
They are not two;
the formless and the formful are one reality."
— *Shankara Vākyamālā*

The Illusion of Multiplicity

The Mystery of the Many

If Brahman alone is real — infinite, unchanging, consciousness itself —
then how do we find ourselves in a world of opposites, motion, and mortality?

How does **the One become the many**?

This question has haunted philosophers across ages.
Shankara's answer is elegant and radical:

"Multiplicity is not a second reality. It is Brahman appearing through Māyā."

Thus, Māyā is not evil, nor false in the moral sense.
It is **the divine power of projection** — the creative self-expression of the Infinite as the finite.

The Nature of Māyā

The Sanskrit root of *Māyā* (���) is *"ma"*, meaning *to measure or limit.*
It is the power that **measures the immeasurable**, making the infinite appear as limited forms.

Shankara calls it *"Anirvachanīyā"* — indescribable.
It is neither real (*sat*) nor unreal (*asat*), but *"mithyā"* — dependent reality, appearing true until knowledge arises.

In his *Brahma Sutra Bhāṣya*, he writes:

"Māyā is beginningless ignorance which projects the manifold universe upon the one Brahman, like the illusion of silver upon mother-of-pearl."

It's not a *thing* but a *tendency* — the universal error of taking appearance for substance.

Rope, Snake, and the Mechanics of Illusion

Shankara's classic metaphor returns:

In twilight, you see a **rope** but mistake it for a **snake**.
You jump in fear, until light reveals the truth.

The snake was never there — yet your experience, your fear, your reaction were real *to you.*

Likewise, the universe, though experientially real, is **ontologically mistaken** — a superimposition (*adhyāsa*) upon the substratum of Brahman.

Once knowledge dawns, the illusion ceases, but nothing is destroyed — because nothing was truly created.

Māyā as Cosmic Dream

To the awakened mind, the world is like a dream: vivid, meaningful, yet ephemeral.

When you dream, your mind projects people, places, events — but on waking, you realize they were all **you**.
Similarly, Brahman dreams the universe, and we are its dream-characters — real within the dream, unreal outside it.

But unlike an individual dream, **Māyā is cosmic** — a shared field of experience that persists until knowledge (*jñāna*) awakens us collectively and individually.

Shankara does not call this dream "bad."
It is **Leela** — the divine play of consciousness discovering itself through form.

Māyā and Avidyā — Macro and Micro Veils

Māyā operates on two scales:

- **Cosmic (Samasti)** — The collective power by which Brahman appears as Īśvara and the universe.
- **Individual (Vyashti)** — The personal ignorance (*Avidyā*) by which consciousness identifies with body and mind.

Thus, what is cosmic illusion in the universe becomes **personal delusion** in the individual.

When Avidyā dissolves, one realizes one's true identity as the Infinite — but Māyā continues for others, just as the dream continues for those still asleep.

The Two Powers of Māyā

Shankara identifies **two aspects** of Māyā that sustain the illusion:

1. **Āvaraṇa Śakti — The Power of Concealment**
    - It veils the reality of Brahman, making us forget our divine nature.
    - Like clouds hiding the sun, it does not destroy light but obstructs our view.
2. **Vikṣepa Śakti — The Power of Projection**
    - It projects multiplicity upon that concealed unity.
    - Names, forms, bodies, desires, and fears arise through this distortion.

Together they create the human condition — the play of ignorance and knowledge, bondage and freedom.

The Function of Māyā — Not Error, but Education

Though Māyā veils truth, it also **guides us toward it**.

Through suffering, contrast, and limitation, we begin to seek what is beyond them.

Thus, Māyā becomes the **matrix of awakening**.

Shankara calls this the *paradox of illusion* — the very force that hides the Absolute also makes the Absolute knowable.

Without illusion, there can be no realization; without darkness, no light.

Māyā, therefore, is **divine pedagogy** — Brahman playing hide-and-seek with itself.

Māyā in the Light of Science

Modern science gives new language to this insight:

- **Quantum theory** shows that the world is not made of solid matter but probability waves observed into existence.
- **Neuroscience** reveals that perception is constructed — we do not see the world "as it is," but as the brain interprets it.
- **Psychology** confirms that memory, emotion, and identity are stories we continually project and believe.

In essence, modern science agrees:

Reality is a **projection of consciousness filtered through measurement — Māyā**.

The ancient seer and the modern physicist stand at the same threshold: the boundary between **appearance and awareness**.

The Purpose of Māyā

If the world is a projection, why does it exist at all?

Shankara answers: **for the play of realization.**

Brahman, being infinite, has no need — yet its nature is *Ānanda* (bliss), which naturally expresses itself.

Creation is not a necessity but a **spontaneous overflow of joy**, like laughter or song.
The universe exists so that the One may behold itself in infinite mirrors.

Thus, life is not a prison of illusion — it is a **drama of awakening**.
Every sorrow, joy, and confusion is part of consciousness remembering itself through experience.

The End of Illusion

Māyā ends not by destruction, but by **understanding**.
When knowledge (*jñāna*) dawns, the distinction between real and unreal dissolves into the knowing that **everything is Brahman**.

The world does not vanish — but its sting does.
One continues to live, act, and love, but with the effortless awareness that it is all divine play.

This is *jīvanmukti* — liberation while living.
To see the rope while the snake still appears is to live freely within the world of Māyā, untouched by it.

The Cosmic Mirror

Imagine infinite mirrors reflecting each other endlessly — each image appearing distinct, yet every reflection containing the whole.

That is the world through Shankara's eyes.
Every form, from atom to galaxy, is a **mirror of Brahman**, reflecting consciousness through the prism of limitation.

To see the One in the many is to transcend illusion without rejecting it.
To see the divine in the mundane — that is the essence of wisdom.

The Awakening from the Dream

When the dreamer awakens, the dream ceases to bind.
But the world of the dream is not denied — it becomes art.

Likewise, when the sage awakens from Māyā, life becomes a **dance of delight**.

Pleasure and pain no longer enslave; they become expressions of the same blissful ground.

"The knower of Brahman, realizing the world as Self,
plays in it like a child — with wonder, not attachment."
— *Shankara, Vivekachūḍāmaṇi*

The Modern Implication — Conscious Creation

Understanding Māyā today is not escapism — it is empowerment.

When you realize the world is projection, you recognize your **creative participation** in it.

Every thought, emotion, and intention shapes your experienced universe.

In this light, *spirituality meets psychology*:

- Awareness dissolves illusion.
- Intention reprograms experience.
- Realization restores unity.

The world is not to be denied, but **reclaimed as divine imagination.**

The Dance of Māyā and Moksha

Māyā does not end with enlightenment; it becomes transparent.

The sage still perceives the world, but sees it as Brahman.

As waves are nothing but water, the universe is nothing but consciousness.

The dance continues — but the dancer has awakened.

"When the seer and the seen are no longer two,
Māyā herself becomes Brahman's laughter."
— *Shankaracharya's Bhāṣya on Māṇḍūkya Kārikā*

Liberation and Self-Realization — End of Seeking

The Journey That Was Never a Journey

All human striving — for wealth, love, power, or peace — is ultimately the search for **wholeness**.

But Shankara unmasks a profound paradox: we seek what we already are.

Liberation (*mokṣa*) is not a state to be attained, but a **truth to be recognized**.

In the *Bhāṣya*, he writes:

"As the rope was ever the rope, even when taken for a snake, so the Self was ever free, even when imagined bound."

Thus, the spiritual journey is circular — it begins in ignorance and ends in the awareness that there was no beginning, no end, and no traveler apart from the destination.

What Is Mokṣa?

Shankara defines *mokṣa* as **the cessation of ignorance and its effects** — not the gaining of a new experience.

It is freedom from:

- **Avidyā (ignorance)** — misidentifying with the non-self (body, mind, ego).
- **Karma (causal bondage)** — being compelled by past impressions.
- **Duḥkha (suffering)** — arising from division, fear, and desire.

When these dissolve, the Self stands revealed as **pure awareness** — infinite, indivisible, self-luminous.

In that state — though "state" is an imperfect word — nothing is added or removed.

Only the **false veil of separation** is lifted.

Jīvanmukti — Liberation While Living

Shankara's *jīvanmukta* is one of humanity's highest ideals: a being liberated **while still embodied**.

Unlike traditions that promise salvation after death, Advaita's enlightenment blooms *here and now.*

The *jīvanmukta* lives as ordinary people do — eats, sleeps, walks, speaks — yet inwardly abides in unbroken awareness of unity.

Pleasure and pain touch the body, but not the being.

"He neither rejoices nor grieves; he dwells as the ocean, unshaken by waves."

— *Bhāṣya on Brahma Sutra 4.1.15*

This is not indifference but **equanimity** — the serenity of one who sees all change as the dance of the changeless.

The Marks of the Liberated One

Shankara describes several qualities that naturally arise in the liberated:

1. **Ānanda** — spontaneous joy, independent of circumstance.
2. **Karuṇā** — compassion born of unity with all beings.

3. **Samatva** — balance amidst opposites.
4. **Svātantrya** — freedom from external validation or dependence.
5. **Śānti** — inner stillness that shines through action.

Such a person does not withdraw from life; rather, life flows through them effortlessly — like wind through an open space.

Knowledge as Liberation

For Shankara, **knowledge (jñāna)** alone is the cause of liberation.

Rituals and good deeds (*karma*) purify the mind, but only knowledge dispels ignorance — just as darkness cannot be swept away, only illumined.

"Action purifies; knowledge liberates."

This *knowledge* is not intellectual accumulation but **direct recognition**:

I am not the doer, not the enjoyer, not the thinker — I am the witness in whom these arise.

When this understanding becomes abiding, the sense of "I" and "mine" dissolves, leaving only **Is-ness**.

The Death of the Ego

The ego (*ahaṅkāra*) is not destroyed but seen through.

It continues as a functional identity — a tool of expression — but loses its claim of ownership.

The sage still says "I," but it no longer refers to a limited person; it points to **universal consciousness**.

This is the ultimate alchemy: turning the lead of individuality into the gold of universality.

In psychological terms, this is the **de-identification from mental narrative** — the same insight toward which transpersonal psychology, depth therapy, and mindfulness point today.

Mirror Analogy — Awareness Without Distortion

Shankara often likens the liberated mind to a **clean mirror**.

It reflects the world perfectly but is untouched by what it reflects.

Pleasure and pain appear as passing images; the mirror remains clear.

Thus, *mokṣa* is not withdrawal from life but participation without attachment — a **lucid engagement** born of freedom.

Modern neuroscience describes similar states as "meta-awareness" — consciousness aware of itself, unentangled in thought or emotion.

The mystic and the scientist converge here.

The Dissolution of Karma

A key question Shankara addresses is: *What happens to karma after realization?*

He answers through the doctrine of the **threefold karma**:

1. **Sañcita** — the accumulated karma of past lives.
2. **Prārabdha** — the portion already ripened to bear fruit in this life.
3. **Āgāmi** — the karma generated by present actions.

For the *jīvanmukta*:

- *Sañcita* is burnt by knowledge.
- *Āgāmi* cannot accrue, as there is no sense of doership.
- *Prārabdha* alone remains until the body falls — like the arrow already released from the bow.

Thus, the sage lives out destiny without bondage — free even in motion.

The Experiential Dimension — Silence Beyond Thought

When asked to describe liberation, Shankara often turns to **silence**.

In the *Bhāṣya on Taittirīya Upanishad*, he says:

"Words return from there, along with the mind, not attaining it."

This silence is not absence; it is the **pregnant fullness of Being** — consciousness aware of itself without object.

It can be glimpsed between thoughts, in deep meditation, or in moments of awe when time seems to stop.

That stillness is not created; it is *remembered* — the ever-present reality behind all movement.

Liberation and the World

To the liberated, the world continues — but as **Brahman in expression**.

Mountains, rivers, people, stars — all shine as Self.

This vision transforms ethics and relationships:

since no one is other, compassion becomes spontaneous, non-moralistic, and joyful.

For Shankara, **Dharma (righteousness)** is not imposed by law but arises from unity.

When one sees oneself in all beings, harm becomes impossible.

The Modern Parallel — Psychological Integration

In contemporary language, liberation is **total integration** — the harmonization of conscious and unconscious, personal and transpersonal.

Where Freud spoke of sublimation, Jung of individuation, and Maslow of self-actualization, Shankara speaks of **Self-realization** — going beyond the personal self altogether.

This is not the perfection of the personality but the **transcendence of personality**.

And yet, the realized person appears fully human — loving, creative, and spontaneous — precisely because they are no longer imprisoned by identity.

The Deathless Awareness

Shankara concludes that the liberated one has discovered the only reality that cannot die — **awareness itself**.
Birth and death belong to the body; beginnings and endings to the mind.

Awareness is the silent witness of them all.
When that is known as one's true nature, the cycle of becoming ends — not by annihilation, but by awakening.

"He who knows, 'I am Brahman,' becomes Brahman indeed — not by union, but by recognition."
— *Bṛhadāraṇyaka Upanishad 1.4.10 (as cited by Shankara)*

The Paradox of the Liberated Life

The *jīvanmukta* lives without motive yet acts with precision; owns nothing yet blesses all;
has no fear of death yet cherishes every breath.

Such a person is not above the world but **transparent to it** — a channel through which Brahman flows freely.
Their life becomes a sermon in silence, their being a mirror of peace.

The End of Seeking

When realization dawns, all spiritual effort ceases naturally.
Meditation, prayer, ritual — they may continue as play, but not as pursuit.
The seeker vanishes into the sought.

This is **the true end of religion** — not disbelief, but direct seeing.
Shankara calls it *Ānanda-svarūpa*: the blissful nature of the Self.

Nothing remains to be attained, because nothing was ever lost.

The search ends not in attainment, but in **awakening to what has always been**.

"When the mind ceases to seek, the heart discovers it was home all along."

— *Inspired by Shankara's Vivekachūḍāmaṇi*

The Radiance of Freedom

The final flowering of Shankara's teaching is *sahaja-samādhi* — the natural state of unbroken awareness amidst daily life.

Here, the sacred and the ordinary are one.

Every breath, every sound, every encounter becomes **Brahman's own celebration**.

This is not transcendence away from the world but **transcendence through it** — the discovery that existence itself is enlightenment.

"The liberated one sees only Brahman — in friend and foe, in gold and clay, in honor and insult.

For him, all is One, all is himself."

— *Bhagavad Gītā Bhāṣya 6.8–9*

Dialogue of Knowledge

The Spirit of Debate

In Shankara's era, India was a **civilization of dialogue**.

Philosophy was not confined to books; it was a living practice — a meeting of minds seeking truth through debate (*vāda*).

In this vibrant intellectual atmosphere, Shankara engaged with every major school — not with hostility, but with respect. He saw opponents not as enemies, but as **perspectives of the same truth**, partially seen.

His mission was not to "win arguments," but to **dissolve partial truths into total vision.**

The Structure of Refutation

Throughout the *Bhāṣya*, Shankara uses a consistent dialectical method:

1. **Pūrvapakṣa** — statement of the opposing view (often with remarkable fairness).
2. **Siddhānta** — presentation of the Advaitic conclusion.
3. **Saṅgati** — logical reconciliation showing how the Upanishads resolve apparent contradictions.

This style is not combative but **synthetic** — a disciplined unfolding of truth through reason and intuition.

Refutation of Materialism (*Lokāyata / Cārvāka*)

The materialists (*Cārvākas*) held that only the physical world is real — that consciousness arises from the elements like the scent from a flower.

Shankara counters:

"That which is not self-luminous cannot illumine itself or others.
Consciousness, being self-revealed, cannot arise from inert matter."

Matter, he says, is known *through* consciousness — never the other way around.
To seek the cause of awareness in the brain or body is like trying to find the sun's light by dissecting its rays.

He doesn't condemn materialism — he elevates it, showing that **matter itself is consciousness appearing as form.**

Modern neuroscience echoes this paradox.
Even today, science cannot explain how subjective experience arises from objective neurons — the so-called *hard problem of consciousness.*
Shankara would smile: the "hard problem" is not in consciousness but in mistaking **appearance for source.**

Refutation of Ritualism (*Pūrva Mīmāṃsā*)

The *Mīmāṃsakas*, devoted to Vedic ritual, argued that liberation comes through precise performance of sacrifices and duties.

Shankara affirms the value of ethical and ritual discipline — but insists they **purify the mind**, not reveal Brahman.

"Action produces results in time; Brahman is timeless.
That which is eternal cannot be attained by the temporal."

He calls ritual the "lower knowledge" (*Apara Vidyā*), necessary but incomplete.

Once the mind is purified, it must turn inward to *Para Vidyā* — direct realization of the Self.

Here, Shankara shifts the axis of spirituality from **doing to knowing** — a revolution in human consciousness.

Refutation of Sāṅkhya Dualism

The **Sāṅkhya** school posited two eternal realities:

- *Puruṣa* — pure consciousness.
- *Prakṛti* — primordial matter.

They held that liberation comes when consciousness recognizes its difference from matter.

Shankara agrees partly: the distinction between the seer and seen is essential — but he goes further.

"If two absolutes exist, one must limit the other.

The infinite cannot coexist with another infinite."

Thus, he shows that **duality collapses into contradiction**.

Consciousness alone exists; matter is its appearance.

The dualism of Sāṅkhya, therefore, is valid as method, but incomplete as metaphysics.

Modern physics, in its turn, dissolves dualities of energy and matter, particle and wave — aligning with Shankara's insight that **all opposites converge in unity.**

Refutation of Buddhism

Shankara's debates with Buddhist philosophers (especially *Mādhyamika* and *Vijñānavāda* schools) were profound and respectful.

He admired the Buddha's insight but clarified where Advaita diverges.

1. **Against Nihilism (Śūnyavāda)** —
   Buddhism's assertion that ultimate reality is void (*śūnya*) is, for Shankara, incomplete.
   He agrees that all forms are empty — but what remains is not *nothingness*; it is **conscious fullness** (*pūrṇatā*).

"The denial of the world does not deny Being;
the negation of form reveals the formless."

1. **Against Subjective Idealism (Vijñānavāda)** —
   Shankara agrees that the world arises in consciousness but rejects that each mind creates its own world.
   Consciousness is not personal but **universal** — the substratum of all.

Thus, where Buddhism ends in the silence of emptiness, Advaita begins in the **silence of fullness**.

Refutation of Theistic Dualism (Dvaita)

Shankara's later critics, like Madhvacharya, would accuse him of denying God.
In truth, Shankara denies *separation*, not *divinity*.

The theists held that God (Īśvara) and the soul (jīva) are eternally distinct — creator and created.
Shankara asks:

"If God is infinite, how can anything exist apart from Him?"

To posit an eternal duality is to limit both.
Thus, Advaita absorbs theism into non-dualism — the wave realizing it has never been other than the sea.

The devotee and the philosopher finally meet in the same silence.

The Art of Integration

Shankara's refutations are **acts of synthesis**, not destruction.
He never dismisses other paths but **repositions** them within the greater unity of Advaita.

- Materialism reveals the outer form.
- Ritualism refines the inner instrument.
- Dualism awakens discrimination.
- Buddhism purifies perception.
  All culminate in the direct recognition of **oneness**.

Each philosophy, he shows, is a rung on the same ladder — the ladder that consciousness ultimately transcends.

The Logic of Non-Dualism

Shankara's reasoning is uncompromisingly clear:

1. Every object of knowledge is known *to* consciousness.
2. Therefore, consciousness cannot be an object — it is the condition of all knowing.
3. What cannot be objectified cannot have a second beside it.
4. Therefore, consciousness alone is real — everything else is appearance within it.

This is the **core logic of Advaita**, where epistemology becomes ontology — knowing and being are one.

The Tone of Compassion

Despite his razor-sharp intellect, Shankara's refutations carry compassion.
He never condemns ignorance as sin but sees it as **forgetfulness** — a veil awaiting dawn.
In his *Bhāṣya on Bhagavad Gītā (4.39)*, he writes:

"By faith, by love, by devotion, by inquiry — the seeker attains knowledge.
And knowledge alone removes sorrow, as sunrise removes darkness."

For him, philosophy is not warfare; it is **illumination through love**.

The Modern Relevance — The End of Ideological Conflict

In our age of polarized ideologies, Shankara's method offers a profound model:
Engage, understand, include, and transcend.

He shows that **truth is not the negation of perspectives, but their reconciliation.**
Science and spirituality, reason and faith, intellect and intuition — all belong to the same dance of consciousness.

Where modern discourse divides, Advaita unites.

The Victory of Clarity

Shankara's debates across India — with Buddhists at Nalanda, ritualists in Mithila, and theists in Kanchipuram — were not political victories but **intellectual liberations**.
His success lay not in defeating others but in **restoring the centrality of realization over ritual, experience over dogma, and unity over fragmentation.**

His refutations were **acts of healing** — restoring philosophy to its original purpose: the direct seeing of truth.

The Sword and the Lotus

Shankara's dialectic is often compared to a **sword** — sharp, precise, cutting through illusion.
But the sword was held in a **lotus hand** — gentle, compassionate, untainted by ego.

He refuted ideas, not individuals; ignorance, not humanity.
For him, the highest argument was **silence born of realization** — the silence where all distinctions melt.

The Triumph of Non-Dual Vision

By the end of his intellectual odyssey, Shankara had unified the scattered currents of Indian thought.
Materialists, ritualists, dualists, and nihilists — all found resolution in his insight that:

"All differences are imagined upon the one consciousness — as ornaments upon gold, as waves upon water."

This vision became India's **spiritual constitution** — the foundation of centuries of art, literature, and mysticism.

And in the modern world, it remains a beacon — the vision of **unity amidst diversity**, the knowing that dissolves all division.

"When the mind sees difference, there is bondage;
when it sees unity, there is liberation."
— *Brahma Sutra Bhāṣya, 2.1.14*

If the earlier chapters described *what Brahman is*, this one reveals *what it feels like to live as Brahman* — a human life radiant with stillness, love, and spontaneous wisdom.

This is the stage where philosophy becomes poetry, and truth becomes life itself.

The State of Oneness — Living as Brahman

From Knowing to Being

In Shankara's Advaita, realization (*jñāna*) is not an intellectual conviction — it is **a shift of identity**.
The seeker no longer says, "I am aware of Brahman," but recognizes, "I *am* Brahman."

This is not arrogance; it is the disappearance of the *false self*. It is awakening from the dream of individuality into the clarity of boundless awareness.

"The knower of Brahman becomes Brahman indeed —
not by transformation, but by recognition."
— *Bṛhadāraṇyaka Upaniṣad Bhāṣya*

In this realization, the old distinctions between *spiritual* and *worldly* dissolve.
There is only the dance of consciousness in infinite forms — peaceful, dynamic, self-knowing.

The Vision of Unity

The liberated one (*jñānī*) perceives the same Self shining through all beings.

Differences of caste, gender, species, or belief vanish in the vision of unity.

"He who sees all beings in the Self,
and the Self in all beings,
does not hate anyone."
— *Īśa Upaniṣad 6 (cited by Shankara)*

To such a one, compassion is not a moral duty; it is the spontaneous fragrance of seeing no other.
Love becomes **ontological** — the natural expression of non-separation.

The Psychology of the Realized One

Shankara describes the *sthita-prajña* — the person of steady wisdom — as one whose mind is tranquil like a windless lake. The waves of desire and fear may ripple on the surface, but the depths remain undisturbed.

Such a person:

- Acts without egoic motive.
- Feels without attachment.
- Thinks without confusion.
- Lives without fear of death.

Modern psychology would call this the **integrated mind**, the state where reactive conditioning ceases and consciousness flows freely — unfiltered, luminous, creative.

The World as Brahman

To the realized mind, the world is not rejected but **re-sacralized**.
Every sound, color, and movement is recognized as the vibration of consciousness itself.

The sage no longer sees multiplicity as fragmentation but as **diversity within unity** — like waves on the ocean or sparks from a fire.

Thus, Shankara's non-dualism is not world-denying but **world-transfiguring**.

He does not preach withdrawal but right vision — *samyag-darśana*.

When the veil of Māyā thins, even the ordinary becomes sacred:

eating, walking, speaking — all become acts of Brahman remembering itself.

The Ethics of Oneness

From the realization of unity arises a natural **ethic of compassion**.

For Shankara, ethics is not imposed by scripture but **emerges from understanding**.

If all beings are the Self, harming another is harming oneself. Thus, *ahimsā* (non-violence) and *dāna* (generosity) are not commandments but consequences of seeing truth.

He writes in the *Bhagavad Gītā Bhāṣya (12.13–14)*:

"The sage is friendly, compassionate, free from possessiveness and ego.

He is equal to friend and foe, content with whatever comes."

Such conduct is not cultivated — it is *effortless rightness* born of vision.

Work Without Doership

Action continues after realization, but **the sense of "I am the doer" disappears.**

Shankara explains:

"For him who knows himself as the witness,
there is no bondage in action,
even as the sky is untouched by clouds."

This is *karma without karma* — action without psychological residue.

The body-mind acts, the world responds, but the Self remains unattached, like the sun reflected in a thousand rivers.

This principle forms the basis of *karma-yoga* — acting from clarity, not compulsion.

The Inner Freedom

The liberated one is **free in all conditions**.
Wealth or poverty, success or failure, praise or blame — none disturb the center of awareness.

This freedom is not detachment born of dullness but **joyful independence** (*svātantrya*).
It is the freedom of the sky — vast enough to contain all weather, yet bound by none.

"The sage neither avoids the world nor clings to it;
he stands in the middle — untouched, unbound, and radiant."
— *Vivekachūḍāmaṇi, 536*

The Deathless Perspective

For the jñānī, death holds no terror.
He knows it as a change of appearance — not the end of consciousness, but its **reconfiguration**.

Shankara says:

"The Self does not die; only the body falls away,
as a traveler leaves a worn-out garment."

In that moment, nothing new happens — only the recognition that nothing ever happened.
The wave merges back into the sea, having never been separate.

Role of Love and Devotion After Realization

Even after realization, **bhakti (devotion)** remains — but its nature changes.
It becomes **love without object** — the overflowing of being for itself.

In his *Saundarya Lahari*, Shankara reveals this tender paradox:

"When I see you within, O Mother,
I cannot see the world;
and when I see the world,
I see only you."

This is devotion *after knowledge* — *parā-bhakti*, love that arises not from longing but from fulfillment.
The lover and the beloved have dissolved into one awareness.

The Liberated in Society

The liberated one does not necessarily withdraw from the world.
Many — like Shankara himself — become teachers, healers, artists, or reformers.

Their presence uplifts silently.
They may appear ordinary, yet their stillness changes those around them — not through persuasion, but **through resonance**.

Shankara notes that such beings are "centers of peace in the world's turbulence,"
embodying a truth beyond preaching.

In modern terms, they are **awakened catalysts** — living reminders of our own infinite potential.

The Modern Parallel — Conscious Evolution

In today's language, living as Brahman means living with **expanded awareness** — perceiving life as a unified field rather than a battlefield of separate selves.

It aligns with contemporary ideas of:

- **Mindfulness** — presence without preference.
- **Flow** — effortless action in harmony with the whole.
- **Nondual psychology** — dissolving the self/other divide.

But Shankara goes beyond — he declares this not a state to achieve, but **the truth of existence already here.**
Conscious evolution, then, is not about becoming divine — it is about realizing we have never been anything else.

The Beauty of Ordinary Life

After realization, even simplicity becomes luminous. Cooking, teaching, listening, or walking — each act glows with awareness.

The mundane and the mystical merge; meditation continues in motion.
This is **sahaja-samādhi** — the spontaneous unity of being.

To live as Brahman is to live in continual wonder —
to look at the sky and see one's own boundlessness reflected there.

The Silence Between Words

Ultimately, the state of oneness cannot be described.
Language divides; realization unites.

Hence Shankara ends many of his commentaries in silence — a pause more eloquent than words.
That silence is the true scripture; all verses merely point toward it.

"In silence is the Supreme revealed —
not by speech, not by mind, not by sight."
— *Kena Upaniṣad Bhāṣya*

Living as Brahman — The Human Flowering

To live as Brahman is not to float above life but to bloom fully within it.
The senses, emotions, and mind remain — but purified of self-centeredness, they become instruments of divine play (*līlā*).

Such a being walks lightly upon the earth, leaves no scar upon time, and carries the fragrance of freedom.

This is **the flowering of humanity into divinity** — not as escape, but as embodiment.

"The liberated one lives in the world as the lotus on water — touching yet untouched, reflecting yet free."
— *Bhagavad Gītā Bhāṣya 5.10*

Legacy of Shankaracharya

The Unbroken Lamp of Wisdom

When Ādi Shankaracharya lived in the 8th century CE, India was a landscape of philosophical diversity — Buddhist logic, ritual orthodoxy, theism, materialism, and countless local traditions.

Into this complexity, he brought **clarity, not conquest**. He did not reject any path — he illuminated its center.

His genius lay not only in intellect but in vision:
he saw through contradiction into the **unity underlying all paths**.
That unity, *Advaita*, became India's inner compass for over a millennium.

Reconciliation, Not Rejection

Shankara harmonized seemingly opposing streams:

- **The Upanishadic mysticism** of non-duality.
- **The ritual precision** of the Vedas.
- **The devotional intensity** of Bhakti.
- **The rational discipline** of logic (*Nyāya*) and philosophy (*Sāṅkhya*).

Each found its place within his integrative vision.
For him, religion without reason was superstition;
reason without realization was emptiness.

This synthesis became the **intellectual and spiritual foundation** of India's renaissance centuries later — influencing saints, poets, reformers, and scientists alike.

Four Maṭhas — Guardians of the Dharma

To ensure that the light of knowledge would never fade, Shankara established **four monastic centers (Maṭhas)** at the four corners of India:

Maṭha	Location	Direction	Presiding Deity	Head Scripture
Sringeri	Karnataka	South	Sharada (Wisdom)	Taittirīya Upaniṣad
Dwaraka	Gujarat	West	Govardhana (Krishna)	Rig Veda
Puri	Odisha	East	Jagannātha	Atharva Veda
Badrinath	Uttarakhand	North	Nārāyaṇa	Sama Veda

These four "pillars of consciousness" preserved not just philosophy but the **continuity of realization** — an unbroken lineage of teachers reminding each generation of the timeless Self.

The Cultural Renaissance of Advaita

Under Shankara's influence, Indian thought underwent a transformation.
He inspired:

- The flowering of **Bhakti literature**, where devotion and non-duality merged (e.g., in the works of Vidyāraṇya, Tulsidas, Kabir).
- The rise of **temple architecture** that reflected cosmic unity — from Sringeri to Kedarnath.
- The resurgence of **Upanishadic study** as the crown of spiritual learning.

He reestablished **spiritual education** not as memorization, but as **self-inquiry** (*ātma-vicāra*).
Through this, he democratized wisdom — teaching that liberation is not for priests or monks alone, but for every human heart ready to awaken.

Shankara's Influence on Later Thinkers

Shankara's vision seeded countless movements of awakening:

- **Ramakrishna and Vivekananda** reinterpreted Advaita for the modern world — "Each soul is potentially divine."
- **Sri Aurobindo** expanded non-duality into a dynamic, evolutionary Advaita — "All life is yoga."
- **Ramana Maharshi** revived direct self-inquiry — "Who am I?" — as the pathless path.
- **J. Krishnamurti**, though rejecting all systems, echoed Shankara's essence — awareness free from the known.

Even in the West, thinkers like **Schopenhauer**, **Aldous Huxley**, **Alan Watts**, and **Erwin Schrödinger** found in Shankara's Advaita a bridge between **science and mysticism**, **reason and revelation**.

Advaita and Modern Science

In our age of physics and neuroscience, Shankara's insights are finding new resonance.

- **Quantum physics** reveals a universe of interconnectivity and observer-dependence — echoing "all is Brahman."
- **Systems theory** and **holistic biology** affirm that life is an indivisible whole, not a collection of parts.
- **Consciousness studies** increasingly recognize awareness as **fundamental**, not derivative.

When Schrödinger declared, "The total number of minds in the universe is one," he was restating Shankara's *ekam eva advitīyam* — "One without a second."

Thus, Advaita is not a metaphysical relic but **the frontier of science meeting spirituality**.

Advaita and Psychology — The Inner Revolution

Modern psychology, too, is catching up with Shankara.
Where Freud spoke of unconscious drives and Jung of archetypes, Shankara spoke of **Avidyā** — ignorance projecting reality.
Where mindfulness teaches witnessing thoughts, Shankara taught **Sākṣī-bhāva** — the state of pure witnessing consciousness.

Transpersonal psychology now confirms what Advaita has always known:
healing lies not in rearranging the mind, but in realizing that **you are not the mind at all.**

Thus, Shankara's teaching becomes the key to **psychological freedom** — the end of inner conflict through the recognition of wholeness.

The Ethical and Ecological Relevance

In a fragmented, divided world, Advaita offers a vision of **interconnected harmony**.

- It dissolves the ego-based nationalism, religious exclusivism, and human-centered arrogance that divide humanity.
- It inspires ecological awareness — seeing the earth, rivers, animals, and sky as **expressions of the same consciousness.**

To live Advaita is to live sustainably, compassionately, and inclusively — to act as the planet itself expressing care through a human form.

Advaita and the Digital Age

Today's information age mirrors Māyā — infinite data, endless forms, constant flux.

Amid this overstimulation, Shankara's clarity is the antidote.

Advaita teaches us to anchor in **Awareness amidst information**,

to use technology as an extension of consciousness, not a substitute for it.

In a world of virtual identities, *"Who am I?"* regains its revolutionary power.

Shankara becomes the philosopher of the post-digital self — reminding us that even in the metaverse, **awareness alone is real.**

The Feminine Face of Advaita

Though often perceived as abstract, Shankara's vision had a deeply **feminine heart**.

His hymns to Saraswati, Tripurasundari, and Annapūrṇa reveal that for him, the formless and the formful are **aspects of the same reality**.

He saw the Divine Mother (*Śakti*) not as separate from Brahman but as **Brahman in motion** — consciousness in creative play.
This integration of wisdom (*jñāna*) and devotion (*bhakti*), intellect and love, forms the foundation for a **holistic spirituality** beyond gender or dogma.

Shankara's Legacy for the Seeker Today

For the modern seeker, Shankara's path remains timeless because it requires no belief — only sincerity.
It invites inquiry, not ideology.
It promises freedom here and now, not in some distant heaven.

His teaching can be distilled into three living principles:

1. **Śravaṇa** — Listening deeply to truth.
2. **Manana** — Reflecting until doubt dissolves.
3. **Nididhyāsana** — Meditating until knowledge becomes being.

Through these, the ancient Upanishadic fire burns anew in every generation.

Advaita as the Future of Human Evolution

Humanity stands today where ancient India once stood — overwhelmed by knowledge, hungry for wisdom.
Advaita offers not escape but **integration** — the end of inner and outer conflict through understanding that all opposites arise in one field of consciousness.

The future of evolution is not technological but **ontological** — the evolution of consciousness itself.
When humanity collectively awakens to its shared essence, science will serve compassion, power will serve peace, and individuality will flower without division.

This is the **Advaitic age** that Shankara foresaw — the spiritual globalization of unity.

The Eternal Presence

Shankara's body perished young, but his awareness never died.
He lives in every sincere question, every moment of stillness, every act of understanding.

His legacy is not a system of thought but a **state of being** —
the luminous silence that underlies all words, all worlds.

As long as a single being asks "Who am I?",
Shankara's spirit will answer, gently, **"Tat Tvam Asi" — Thou art That.**

"Brahman alone is real, the world is appearance,
the Self is not different from Brahman."
— *Shankara's Mahāvākya Summary*

The Infinite Continuum

The *Brahma Sutra Bhāṣya* began with a call — *"Now, therefore, the inquiry into Brahman."*
It ends not with conclusion but **continuation** — the inquiry that becomes life itself.

For Shankara, knowledge was not the end of questioning, but the flowering of perpetual wonder.
To live Advaita is to live as that wonder — aware, alive, and free.

"There is no liberation apart from this knowing:
that I am the one consciousness in all beings.
Knowing this, the sage rests in peace."
— *Brahma Sutra Bhāṣya, 4.4.21*

Epilogue: The Living Flame

When Shankara climbed the Himalayas and disappeared into legend,
he left behind not ashes, but a **living flame** —
a vision that unites intellect and intuition, love and logic, self and cosmos.

That flame burns still — in monasteries and modern minds,
in science labs and meditation halls,
in every heart that dares to awaken.

For wherever truth is sought,
Shankara walks again —
not as a man, but as awareness itself.

About the Author

Dr. Surabhi Solanki is an author and thinker whose work brings the timeless clarity of Advaita Vedanta into the consciousness of the modern reader. Her writings illuminate the essential teachings of ancient India with a voice that is both rooted in tradition and attuned to contemporary spiritual inquiry.

Before dedicating herself fully to authorship and publishing, she practiced as a homeopathic physician—an experience that shaped her sensitivity to the subtle dimensions of human suffering and the universal search for wholeness. Over time, her path drew her inward, toward the world of the Upanishads, the Bhagavad Gita, and the profound commentaries of Adi Shankaracharya. What began as a personal exploration unfolded into a lifelong calling: to translate, interpret, and present classical wisdom in a way that speaks to the present age.

Her books—including Divine Truth Unveiled (Mandukya Karika), Bhagavad Gita: Insights from Adi Shankaracharya, Essence of Yoga Vasistha, Power Beyond Perception (Kena Upanishad), Awakening Through Vedanta, and The Hidden Secrets of Immortality (Katha Upanishad Retold)—have earned her recognition among seekers who value clarity, depth, and intellectual honesty.

In this volume, Brahma Sutra Bhāṣya: Shankaracharya's Defining Work — A Modern Retelling, she brings her characteristic approach—a blend of philosophical rigor, intuitive insight, and contemplative sensitivity—to one of the most challenging and foundational texts of Vedanta. Her intention is not to reinterpret Shankara, but to bring his uncompromising vision into a language that can be understood, reflected upon, and lived.

Dr. Solanki's body of work reflects her belief that spiritual knowledge is not reserved for scholars alone. It is meant for anyone who has ever questioned the nature of reality, the meaning of existence, or the source of the "I" that witnesses all experience. Through her books, she invites readers to discover the inner certainty that Shankaracharya called the Self—pure, limitless, and ever-free.

She continues to write, publish, and mentor readers around the world who seek a direct, experiential understanding of truth. Her mission is simple but profound: to make the wisdom of the sages accessible to every sincere seeker, and to support the awakening of clarity in a world that needs it more than ever.

Official Website: drsurabhisolanki.com

Email: drsurabhisolanki@gmail.com

www.ingramcontent.com/pod-product-compliance
Ingram Content Group UK Ltd.
Pitfield, Milton Keynes, MK11 3LW, UK
UKHW021342190726
13845UKWH00027B/684

9 789356 263598